WORKING TOGETHER: Economy, Technology, and Careers in Israel

VOICES FROM ISRAEL

Elisa Silverman

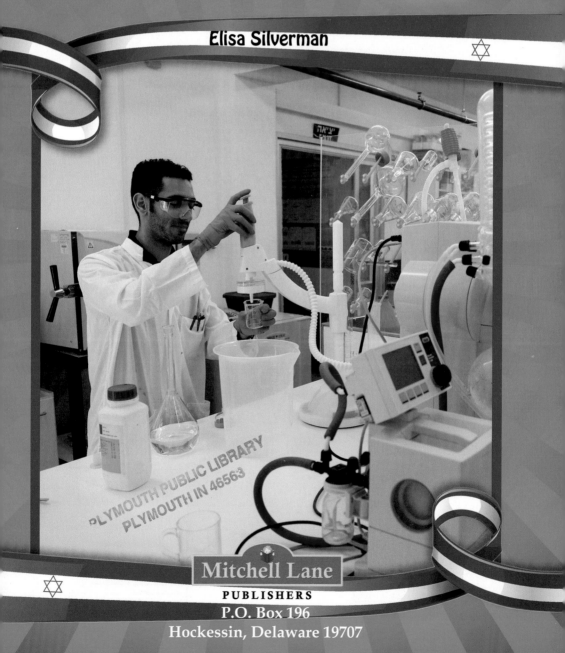

Mitchell Lane
PUBLISHERS
P.O. Box 196
Hockessin, Delaware 19707

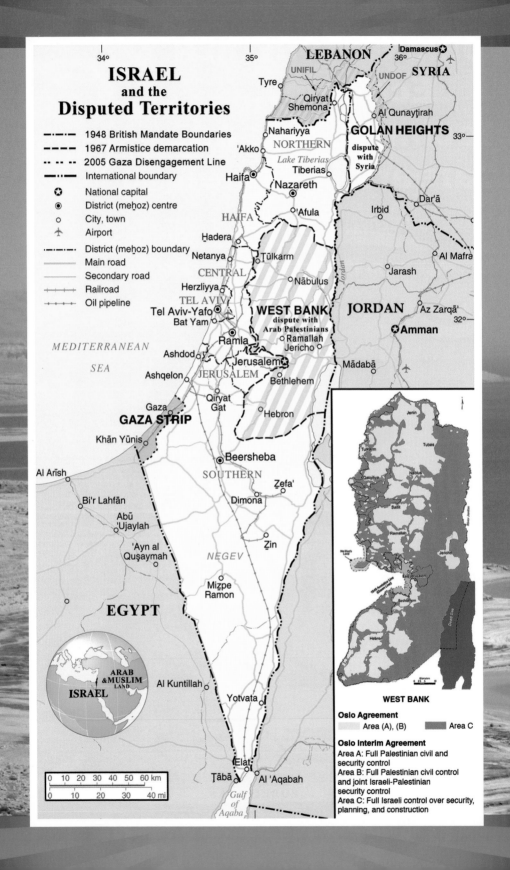

ISRAEL
and the
Disputed Territories

-·-·-	1948 British Mandate Boundaries
- - -	1967 Armistice demarcation
··· ···	2005 Gaza Disengagement Line
-··-··-	International boundary
✪	National capital
◉	District (meḥoz) centre
○	City, town
✈	Airport
-·-·-	District (meḥoz) boundary
──	Main road
──	Secondary road
++++	Railroad
·+·+·	Oil pipeline

LEBANON
UNIFIL
Damascus ✪
SYRIA
UNDOF

Tyre ○
Qiryat Shemona ○
Al Qunayţirah ○
GOLAN HEIGHTS
dispute with Syria
Nahariyya ○
NORTHERN
'Akko ○
Lake Tiberias
Tiberias ○
Dar'ā ○
Haifa ◉
Nazareth ◉
Irbid ○
HAIFA
'Afula ○
Al Mafra ○
Ḥadera ○
Netanya ○
Ṭūlkarm ○
Jarash ○
CENTRAL
Nābulus ○
Herzliyya ○
TEL AVIV
WEST BANK
dispute with Arab Palestinians
JORDAN
Az Zarqā' ○
Tel Aviv-Yafo ◉
Bat Yam ○
Ramallah ○
✪ Amman
Ramla ◉
Jericho ○
MEDITERRANEAN
SEA
Ashdod ○
Jerusalem ◉
Mādabā ○
Ashqelon ○
JERUSALEM
Bethlehem ○
Gaza ○
Qiryat Gat ○
Hebron ○
GAZA STRIP
Khān Yūnis ○
Al Arīsh ○
Beersheba ◉
SOUTHERN
Zefa' ○
Bi'r Lahfān ○
Dimona ○
Abū 'Ujaylah ○
Zin ○
'Ayn al Quşaymah ○
NEGEV
Mizpe Ramon ○
EGYPT
Al Kuntillah ○
Yotvata ○
ISRAEL
ARAB & MUSLIM LAND
Elat ○
✈
Ṭābā ○
Al 'Aqabah ○
Gulf of Aqaba
Jordan

34° 35° 36° 33° 32°

0 10 20 30 40 50 60 km		
0 10 20 30 40 mi		

WEST BANK

Oslo Agreement
Area (A), (B)   Area C

Oslo Interim Agreement
Area A: Full Palestinian civil and security control
Area B: Full Palestinian civil control and joint Israeli-Palestinian security control
Area C: Full Israeli control over security, planning, and construction

Mitchell Lane
PUBLISHERS

Printing　　　1　　　2　　　3　　　4　　　5　　　6　　　7　　　8　　　9

Library of Congress Cataloging-in-Publication Data
Silverman, Elisa, author.
　Working together : economy, technology, and careers in Israel / by Elisa Silverman.
　　pages cm — (Voices from Israel)
　Includes bibliographical references and index.
　Summary: "Written by an author who lives in Israel, this book gives kids from other parts of the world insight into the economy, technology, and careers in Israel today. The Israeli economy has its earliest roots in socialist ideology, but over the years it has taken a more free-market approach to its development. The core Israeli character of creativity, directness, and a willingness to take risks inspires the country's economic progress. Despite few natural resources and hostile countries, Israelis have built a strong economy that provides the world with some of its most cutting edge technology. Israeli innovation is evident in fields from mobile and Internet technologies to science which improves access to food and water around the globe. However, not all Israelis have found their place in this vibrant workforce. Because Israel understands its most vital natural resource is its people, the country is working to expand economic opportunity and extend the entrepreneurial spirit with all its citizens:— Provided by publisher.
　ISBN 978-1-61228-679-2 (library bound)
1. Israel—Economic conditions—Juvenile literature. 2. Economic development—Israel—Juvenile literature. I. Title.
　DS102.95.S578 2015
　330.95694—dc23
　　　　　　　　　　　　　　　　　　　　　　　　　　　　　　2015003197
eBook ISBN: 978-1-61228-688-4

ABOUT THE COVER: Israel is a world leader in developing technologies to improve access to water. Here, researchers at Ben-Gurion University treat water filter membranes using an inkjet printer to improve the filter's ability to prevent bacteria growth in water.

PUBLISHER'S NOTE: This story is based on the author's extensive research and knowledge of Israel, which she believes to be accurate. Documentation of such research is contained on pp. 59–61.

　The Internet sites referenced herein were active as of the publication date. Due to the fleeting nature of some web sites, we cannot guarantee they will all be active when you are reading this book.

PRONUNCIATION NOTE: The author has included pronunciations for many of the Hebrew words in this book. In these pronunciations, the letters "ch" are not pronounced like the "ch" in "children." Instead, the letters "ch" represent the Hebrew letter chet, which sounds like a "kh" or hard "h" sound, similar to the "ch" in "Loch Ness Monster."

PBP

CONTENTS

BOLD words in text can be found in the glossary

Introduction

The Bible describes the Land of Israel as flowing with milk and honey. Yet, in the twenty-first century, Israel could just as well be described as a land flowing with new technologies. What is the force responsible for that transformation? It could be described as *chutzpah* (CHOOTS-pah), a **Yiddish** word that may be roughly translated to mean an attitude of nervy daring. Perhaps that is the best word to describe the adventure of a people who decided to return to its homeland after 2,000 years of exile and managed to create an independent state in 1948.

Today, Israel is home to Jews from all over the world. Israel's citizens work together to develop a country known for its advanced technologies. Israel has a vibrant economy and consistently ranks as one of the world's most competitive economies by global organizations, with particularly high marks for creativity and **entrepreneurship**.[1] Israelis are also the most active users of social media in the world[2] and there are more cell phones in Israel than there are people.[3] Only the United States and China have more companies traded on **NASDAQ** than Israel.[4]

None of this could have been predicted when Israel was founded in 1948. In the early days, many of Israel's founders had the vision of a modern state linked to its ancestral land through agriculture. At the time, Israel's **Zionist** founders included many political leaders deeply influenced by **socialism**. Although socialist ideology no longer holds sway and agriculture is much less dominant, the daring spirit and culture of those times have helped Israel to meet the challenge of twenty-first century economic development and high technology.

The purist symbol of socialist ideology in Israel was the *kibbutz* (key-BOOTZ). "Kibbutz" comes from the Hebrew word for "group." This was the name given to a group of people who chose to be part of a shared agricultural community guided by the vision of creating an ideal socialist society. Only a small proportion of Israelis live on kibbutzim (the Hebrew plural for kibbutz), yet the ideology of communal living and shared responsibility has made an important contribution to Israeli culture.

In the early days of the kibbutz, members rotated jobs, one day working in the fields, the next in the laundry, and the day after in the kibbutz office. There was no private property and the kibbutz owned everything—even the clothes! Kibbutz members are called "kibbutznikim," the Hebrew plural for kibbutznik, a person who belongs to a kibbutz. When kibbutznikim would send their dirty clothes to the laundry, they would receive clean clothes in the right size, though not necessarily the same clothes they had worn earlier. All daily activities were also done as a group. Individuals and families did not have kitchens or dining rooms in their homes. The kibbutznikim ate all their meals together in a communal dining room. Children didn't live with their parents, but in children's dormitories.

Aside from the kibbutz, the most important of the socialist Zionist organizations was the *Histadrut* (hees-TAH-droot), a trade union established in 1920. By 1927, three-quarters of the Jewish workforce in **Mandatory Palestine** were members.[5] The Histradrut was more than a trade union organized to support workers. It was a major player in the Israeli economy. The Histradrut owned companies and dominated many industries. It worked closely with the Israeli government, which was dominated by the socialist Labor party until the late 1970s.

Events such as the Six-Day War in 1967 and a financial crisis in the 1980s helped push the country away from socialist influences. However, there is an irony in that transformation. Many of the traits that led Israel to focus on technology and create a twenty-first century **capitalist** economy have their roots in the early Zionist culture which was so strongly drawn to socialism. This book invites you to take a look at the institutions, culture and people who are shaping Israel's economic and technological achievements. Then, as now, Israel's most important resource is its people. In the words of Israel's past President, Shimon Peres, "The only capital at [Israel's] disposal was our human capital."[6]

Guard duty remains an important job on every kibbutz. Here, a kibbutznik does her part in 1936.

CHAPTER 1
The Enduring Values of the Kibbutz

Nervy daring, or chutzpah, combines two traits: an **audacious** vision and the willingness to take major action to realize that vision. The early Zionist pioneers, including Labor Zionists and others, shared the audacious vision of re-establishing the Jewish state, and they were willing to take big risks and invest the hard work to make it happen. This shared audacious vision enabled them to take on a mission they believed was for the benefit of an entire nation. They were also unafraid to experiment with the new ideas of the time, such as socialism.

The Zionist pioneers of Israel also valued strong community ties and social equality. This bred an informality in Israeli social connections that allows for the direct, honest communication that other cultures may find abrasive. Zionist ideology did not breed a sense of obedience or a submissive attitude to titles and hierarchies. In the army or in the office, Israelis freely challenge each other and authority. In Israeli society, a high military rank or a fancy corporate title is no shield against hard questions or the demand for accountability—which can be posed by anyone.

These pioneers had courage, purpose, and strong social bonds. But they needed more than that to build a new country on a land with no natural resources flanked by many enemies. They needed creativity. Their circumstances forced them to take on big problems, such as how to grow crops on inhospitable land and with little water. Or how to fight wars and build a defense force with broken-down, second-hand military equipment.

"There is no choice," or in Hebrew, "*Ayn breyra*" (ain bray-RAH) is one of Israel's unofficial mottos. Solutions must be found.

The need to overcome challenges required innovative thinking, and reinforced both the will—and the necessity—to take risks. Through trial and error, Israel's founders learned that failure was an important step in learning, which ultimately leads to success. So having an idea or a business that fails isn't counted as mark against you—as long as you learn from it.

The Values that Shape Israel's Move to a Free Market Economy
The nature of Israel's economy has changed greatly over the years, yet core Israeli values have not changed. In fact, those values have contributed to the economy's transformation. Kibbutzim represent the socialist ideology that influenced Israel's society and economy, so it is instructive to look at the way Israel's core values influenced the kibbutz movement and the move toward a more free market system.

The commitment of Israelis to strong social ties begins with the smallest unit—the family. This was no less true on the kibbutzim. The socialist ideal said that the children belonged to the entire community. This was the reason that kibbutzim chose to separate the children's living quarters from their parents.

By the 1970s, parents on kibbutzim began pressing their communities to allow their children to live with them, so they could raise their sons and daughters in their own homes.

A greater focus on family units forced kibbutzim to take a very different approach to the design of living spaces. Families wanted to have some of their meals at home, instead of always eating in the communal dining room. Thus kitchens and dining rooms were added to the family homes built on the kibbutzim. This shift back to a more family-centered social unit sparked the re-thinking of public and private space.

The traditional kibbutz also controlled many aspects of the personal lives of its members: where they learned and the subjects they studied, their work place, and when and where they vacationed. Young adults born and raised on the kibbutz felt their choices were limited, and began to leave the kibbutzim in large numbers during the 1970s. They left to seek individual identity and opportunity.

In the 1980s, all of Israel coped with very difficult economic times, including **hyperinflation**. The kibbutzim suffered added economic challenges. The people of Israel elected the country's first right-wing, free-market oriented government in 1977. Led by Prime Minister Menachem Begin of the **Likud Party** (lee-KOOD), the new Israeli government brought to an end many of the benefits kibbutzim had received from the state, such as special tax breaks, subsidies, and government contracts. While the kibbutzim were granted a bail-out during this financial crisis, they realized this was a one-time pardon.[1]

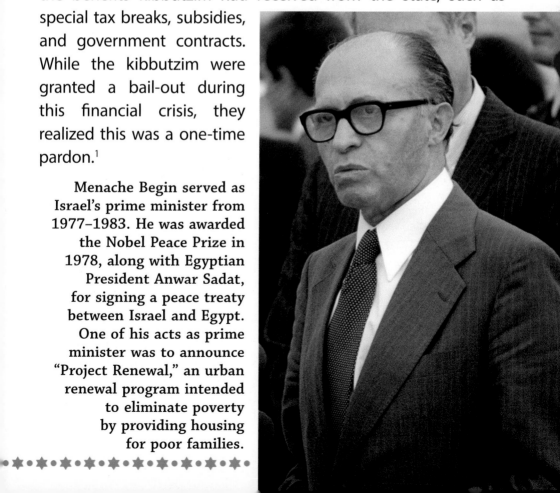

Menache Begin served as Israel's prime minister from 1977–1983. He was awarded the Nobel Peace Prize in 1978, along with Egyptian President Anwar Sadat, for signing a peace treaty between Israel and Egypt. One of his acts as prime minister was to announce "Project Renewal," an urban renewal program intended to eliminate poverty by providing housing for poor families.

A group of young kibbutzniks from the 1950s enjoy a trip to the Mediterranean Sea with their teachers. During this era of the Kibbutz Movement, children lived in children's dormitories away from their parents, where they studied, played, and slept. Often a group of children would stay with the same teacher and caretakers from first grade until seventh grade.

A kibbutz dining hall, circa 1968–1972. At this time, all kibbutz members still ate together in a communal dining room, which was also an important social center.

A view of the Merom Golan Kibbutz in northern Israel. Since the kibbutz is located in beautiful natural surroundings, and one of the rare places in Israel to expect snow in the winter, one of the kibbutz's main businesses is tourism.

So in true Israeli fashion, the kibbutznikim didn't shy away from taking a hard, honest look at their new situation. They experimented with a variety of new and different approaches to becoming financially sustainable. There was no one solution that could be applied to all the kibbutzim in order to achieve self-sufficiency. Each kibbutz found its own path, with some quicker than others to move away from the socialist ideal.

Kibbutzim expanded into non-agricultural industries, from plastics manufacturing to tourism. They hired foreign workers. They ended job rotation so the individual members could develop and contribute in keeping with their individual talents. Some kibbutznikim even began to work for employers outside their home kibbutz. Perhaps the most radical departure from socialist roots was the decision of some kibbutzim to pay their members in accordance with their skills and productivity, rather than giving out allowances on the basis of the kibbutz's judgment of its members needs.

A Country of Immigrants

Another important group of Israeli citizens were also on the move—immigrants from other countries. Immigrants to Israel, called *olim* (oh-LEEM), already demonstrated their willingness to make a big move and take risks, like the Israelis who preceded them. The straight talk and direct questions of the long-time Israelis may have required new immigrants to adjust their expectations of social mores. But they were motivated by the same sense of purpose that led the early pioneers to establish a modern Jewish State on the ancient Jewish homeland. These immigrants from across the globe discovered their shared social bond—whether they were from Europe, the Americas, Russia, Africa, or the countries of the Middle East and the Mediterranean.

TWENTY-FIRST CENTURY KIBBUTZ

The kibbutz movement celebrated its 100-year anniversary in 2010. The first kibbutz in Israel was Kibbutz Degania. It was founded in 1910 on the southern tip of the Kinneret. In 2007, the kibbutz was privatized. This meant that kibbutz members would now receive salaries for their work on the kibbutz, based on the market value of their contribution. Members who receive a salary for employment beyond the kibbutz were no longer required to give their income to the kibbutz. Members also had to begin to pay for many services once provided by the shared funds of the kibbutz.

There are some 270 kibbutzim in Israel today.[2] Less than a quarter of them still adhere to the socialist, communal economy, but they all give high priority to the community's social bonds.[3] There are even some urban kibbutzim. After a period of declining membership, there are now 120,000 Israelis who are members of kibbutzim, the greatest number of people active in the kibbutz movement in its history.[4]

Kibbutz Degania Alef

Students from Jerusalem's Shuafat Al-Touri Arab high school working in the laboratory at Hebrew University's Givat Ram campus. The laboratory includes facilities for learning and experimenting in the fields of biology, chemistry, physics, and computers. Through special programs, the university makes the laboratory available to a limited number of high schools students.

CHAPTER 2
The Challenge of Opening the Door to Fuller Employment

If Israel's people are its greatest resource, this resource isn't being used to its fullest. The country has a relatively low labor participation rate, that is, the percentage of people of working age who actually work. That figure is 63.6 percent.[1] The average labor participation rate in countries that are members of the **Organization for Economic Cooperation and Development** (OECD) is 66 percent.[2] The average Israeli worker spends 1,890 hours a year working, which is 114 hours more than the average worker in an OECD country.[3] Yet those work hours are generally less productive.[4]

Israel has a robust and dynamic economy, even if a high proportion of its people are not participating. Israel's **gross domestic product** (GDP) is $258.1 billion,[5] and is on track to continue growing at a rate above three percent per year.[6] That makes Israel's economic growth rate higher than the average growth rate in OECD countries.

This raises a question: How can a workforce create a sturdy economy and underperform at the same time?

The answer is found when one considers education—and who works and who does not work.

The Impact of Higher Education
On the whole, Israel is a very well-educated country. Nearly half the adult population has an advanced degree.[7] Those with at least a bachelor's degree make up 83 percent of the adult

population.[8] There is little difference between men and women in terms of their education levels.[9] Overall unemployment in Israel is quite low at five percent.[10] Here again, there is little difference between men and women,[11] although unemployment rates do vary in keeping with the individual's level of education.[12]

There are two communities in Israel that are not in sync with these educational statistics: The ultra-Orthodox, or *Haredi* (ha-ray-DEE) Jewish communities, and Israel's Arab communities. These communities have the lowest participation rates in the Israeli labor force, primarily because only one adult in the household is likely to work. In the typical Israeli family, both parents work. Roughly 20 percent of Israeli households live under the poverty level, and in most of these households, only one adult is employed.[13]

The situation may be explained by a number of issues. The ultra-Orthodox Jews educate their children in religious schools. The schools offer limited secular studies, so their education does not adequately prepare them to join the workforce. In the Arab communities, schools do not receive the same government resources as the Jewish schools. In Arab society, women are less likely to be part of the workforce, and if they do, they tend to be employed close to home.

Large proportions of ultra-Orthodox men pursue religious studies rather than participate in the workforce. These circumstances require ultra-Orthodox women to work both inside and outside the home. However, their lack of secular education often leaves them without the skills to qualify for well-paying jobs. In addition, neither the ultra-Orthodox nor Arabs serve in the Israeli army, known as the Israel Defense Force (IDF), in high numbers. As you'll read in the next chapter, military service has a great impact on one's future career.

Israel is the smallest country in the world to launch its own satellites into space. The Israel Space Agency launched the country's first satellite, the Ofek 1, on September 19, 1988. It launched the Ofek 10 in mid-2014, making it Israel's seventh satellite currently in orbit. Israel has satellites to serve commercial and security purposes. "Ofek" is Hebrew for "horizon."

How to Expand Participation in Israel's Workforce?

The governor of the Bank of Israel has made it quite clear. Dr. Karnit Flug has said that Israel "will pay a heavy economic and social price in the years to come" if the ultra-Orthodox and Arab communities aren't brought into the labor force.[14] The Israeli economy and society can't achieve its full potential without the active participation of both groups in the workforce.

She explains that a society with groups that have such a low rate of employment can cut the country's expected economic growth rate by 1.3 percent.[15] The Bank of Israel has also projected that if the education of both groups is brought into line with the rest of the Israeli population, economic growth over the next 50 years will be five percent higher than it would be otherwise.[16]

Israel has been working to address this issue. The Israeli government and other organizations have been working together to improve the quality of education in Arab schools and expand career opportunities. A number of projects focus on launching and supporting Arab entrepreneurs, including some projects specifically designed to encourage Arab women to start their own businesses and work outside their villages. There are also a number of initiatives designed to encourage haredi men to pursue vocational training and higher education to enter the workforce.

Since human capital is Israel's most critical resource, investing in the success of its entire population is the best guarantee of continued success for the nation.

SALARIES

Among those who do work, education level often has a direct impact on salary. The average Israeli monthly salary is approximately NIS 9,000 (that is, New Israeli Shekels), about $2,570 (if the conversion rate is $1=3.8 New Israeli Shekels). However, half of Israelis earn considerably less.[17] The outcome is that one segment of the Israeli workforce earns quite a bit more than the rest.

For example, technology and financial professionals can earn between NIS15,000–25,000 a month. Individuals employed by powerful unions, such as port workers and electricity company workers also tend to earn high salaries. In contrast, a recent study found that in certain sectors of the economy workers may not even be earning Israel's minimum monthly wage as required by law—NIS 4,300.[18] These low wages were most often found in the hospitality, agriculture, health, and welfare services sectors.[19]

A Palestinian worker manufacturing furniture for an Israeli company

A forklift operator moving cargo at Kerem Shalom crossing

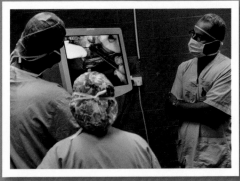

Israeli physicians watching heart surgery

An Israeli marine biologist uses a special instrument to check the eggs of a live female sturgeon

Young people from around the world celebrate their graduation from the IDF's Marva program at the Kotel in Jerusalem. Marva provides an opportunity to non-Israelis to experience the rigors and joys of life in the IDF and in Israel.

CHAPTER 3
MANDATORY SERVICE IN THE IDF—The Army Means Business

A significant part of Israel's investment in its people occurs during their military service. As teenagers approach high school graduation, they begin to vie for their roles in the Israel Defense Forces, where most citizens are obligated to serve. They face fierce competition, as they take exam after exam and undergo many interviews. In the Israel Defense Forces, most interviews and tests take place during one very intense day.

High school students receive their *tzav rishon* (tzahv ree-shown), or "first notice." This notice tells them when and where they're to go to the recruitment center for their day of tests and interviews. The students take medical, psychological, and mental aptitude exams. They are interviewed individually. Young men who have a profile that qualifies them for combat units go through a second interview. The IDF also assigns them an overall score based on all the tests and interviews. The IDF doesn't release anyone's score. It's used by the IDF to decide each person's classification and profile, which determines which jobs and roles they can be assigned. A teenager is given a profile after the first round of testing, and then applicants who qualify for combat or other elite units are invited for additional interviews and try-outs. The teenagers go through the entire process with the hope of being accepted to the military unit of their choice.

A soldier's military unit and job assignment have a direct impact on his or her employment prospects after military service is complete. Even though future employers don't have access to the IDF test results, they understand the selection and training process. As a result, employers use military experience as a measuring stick to compare job applicants, and to determine whether their skills match their company's needs. In some cases, job notices may even specify the employer's preference for applicants who have served in certain military units.

The Intangibles
Assignments to military units and jobs provide soldiers with a great deal of practical training and skills. However, the experience of being in the military also gives the young men and women intangible skills, which have proven highly useful to Israel's economy.

Responsibility and Resourcefulness
The IDF has a very low ratio of officers to rank-and-file soldiers. This means that very young soldiers have a lot of responsibility to make decisions, including tough and swift decisions that bear an impact on a large number of people. Because they are given so much responsibility, soldiers learn to be resourceful.

For example, helicopter tail blades were once used as a "flying lawn mower."[1] During the 2006 Lebanon War, a 20-year old helicopter pilot was called upon to pull a wounded soldier off the battlefield. The wounded soldier was on a stretcher surrounded by bushes. The bushes prevented the helicopter from reaching the wounded soldier. What could the pilot do? He used the tail blades to cut away the bushes so he could get his helicopter to hover low enough to the ground and reach the wounded soldier to pull him onto the helicopter. This story is told in the book Start-Up Nation, where the authors note that using a helicopter this way probably isn't generally recommended.

Teamwork and Critical Reviews

In Israeli society, the IDF is also seen as a great social equalizer. People from different backgrounds live and serve together. These include secular and religious Jews from all economic levels and ethnic backgrounds as well as Israel's non Jewish minorities, including **Druze** and **Bedouins**. On a practical level, everyone needs to learn to work together. Team work is vital to completing a shared mission. Because lives are dependent on cooperation, teamwork also requires questioning each move to

Soldiers in the Givati Brigade complete the final leg of one of the IDF's famed commando courses: the stretcher run. During the multi-day course, soldiers march through the Jerusalem mountains, carrying between 50 pounds to half their own body weight in equipment, and performing various tasks. The Givati Brigade is under IDF's Southern Command. It's one of the oldest infantry brigades in the IDF, dating back to the War of Independence in 1948. Today, it is stationed near Gaza, where it conducts anti-terror operations.

Heavy military transport helicopter Sikorsky CH-53

The IDF uses a range of different types of artillery, from unguided curve trajectory shells to the highly-sophisticated Tammuz missile. The Tammuz missile carries a camera in its tip, which allows it to be steered in flight.

Israel Air Force Kfir C2 fighter jet

664

An Israeli soldier carrying a tear gas gun

IDF soldiers with the Tavor rifle. The Tavor, which was developed specifically for the IDF, is the standard issues weapon for a number of IDF units.

make sure the best decisions are made. Tough questions and reviews after a mission are also essential to the process.

As a result, social bonds among unit members are very strong and grow even stronger after compulsory army service is concluded. After Israelis finish their compulsory military service, all the men and some women continue to do reserve duty, called *miluim* (mee-loo-eem). Reserve units are composed of the same people who first served in the IDF together as young adults. So it's not uncommon for people who served together to assist each other professionally throughout their careers.

In fact, there are a couple of military units that are quite famous for churning out army buddies who become entrepreneurs together.

We're All in the Same Business Now

While a good military record is a critical stepping stone into the workforce, there are two IDF units particularly known for making an outsized contribution to Israel's broad technology sector.

The Influence of Military Intelligence: Unit 8200

Founded in 1952, Unit 8200 is part of the IDF's Military Intelligence. It gathers huge collections of electronic intelligence. Members of the unit develop complex **algorithms** to sort through data to find and track potential enemies of Israel. As former members have explained: Once you've developed programs to identify patterns and predict behavior of potential suicide bombers, using the same skills to identify credit risks or select clothes for consumers isn't so difficult.[2]

Today, Unit 8200 alumni are among the staff of practically every technology company in Israel.[3] One former member has said, "More high-tech billionaires were created from Unit 8200 than from any business school in the country."[4] Indeed, when a few Unit 8200 veterans begin or join a company, they tend to seek out other Unit 8200 veterans because of their confidence in the quality of training and creativity of their fellow unit members.

The existence of this military unit was only recently acknowledged publicly, but it now has a formal "Unit 8200 Alumni Association" for networking. The unit also sponsors hacking contests for high school students (under strict supervision, of course) to help students develop their skills and to enable the unit to identify potential recruits.

The Israel Air Force (IAF) also provides some of the most prestigious assignments in the IDF, easing the transition to civilian work life. Here, two majors in the IAF monitor images sent back by unmanned aerial vehicles (UAVs). Israel uses UAVs to take photos so it can stay on top of both internal and external security in real time. They keep an eye on Jerusalem's light rail, often a target of terror attacks. Some larger UAVs are also equipped with missiles, in addition to cameras.

Talpiot: Combining Higher Education with Military Service

Being a member of the elite *Talpiot* (tahl-pee-oat) unit means committing to serving in the IDF for nine years, six years longer than most standard IDF service. Even so, the unit invites only the top two percent of all high school students to apply.[5] In this group, only 10 percent pass the first round of screening.[6] At the end of the process, perhaps 60 high school students are accepted.[7]

The Talpiot unit members are the IDF's scientists. They go through the same basic training as general soldiers, but they also study all branches of science. The first three-and-a-half years of military service are dedicated to earning academic degrees in mathematics and physics. Then they continue to study, research, and work in other sciences, like biology, computer science, or electrical engineering.

The goal is to cultivate engineers and scientists who have a broad and deep understanding of all the sciences so they can be as creative as possible in their research for the IDF. One former Talpiot member explains it this way: While some problem-solvers look to see what tool in their toolbox will work best—members of Talpiot examine situations to dream up the tools that need to be created.[8]

Talpiot has also produced its fair share of technology company leaders, particularly in the life sciences. The idea for the unit began with Air Force Brigadier General Aharon Beth-Halachmi (ah-HAH-rown beth-hah-LACH-me). He credits the success of the unit to "a stringent selection and testing process to identify boys and girls who are not only gifted scholastically but are also creative, idealistic, resolute and demonstrate leadership."[9]

UNIVERSAL CONSCRIPTION

Serving in the IDF may be a means to a good career, but it's also a great burden with a high level of risk attached. For this reason, the majority of Israelis who serve in the IDF are impatient with the ultra-Orthodox who don't serve in the IDF. Although many religious Jews do serve, most ultra-Orthodox Israelis do not—instead, they continue their studies in religious academies and are exempt from military service.

In 2014, a law requiring the ultra-Orthodox to "share a larger part of the social burden"[10] of army service was passed by the Knesset. The law gradually reduces the number of religious exemptions allowed and would place criminal sanctions on those who avoid military duty. In early 2015, four Haredi men spent a month in prison after they refused to show up at the army recruitment center when called. During protests against the detentions and the law, roughly 50 ultra-Orthodox men were arrested.

Thus the Universal Conscription law remains one of Israel's most divisive and combative social issues. The future existence of the law is in question as it's become an issue in the 2015 government elections.

Religious IDF soldiers praying at the Kotel, including one wearing a tallit (TAH-leet), a traditional Jewish prayer shawl, and tefillin (teh-FILL-in), small black boxes that contain Torah verses and are strapped to the head and the arm during prayer. Among them stands a young Haredi man, who may one day be called to serve in the IDF with them.

Crops get watered on an Israeli farm.

CHAPTER 4
Making the Desert Bloom

When Zionist pioneers began to arrive in the Land of Israel in the late nineteenth century, it was not ripe for agricultural development. There was little water. The land was either too salty, too rocky, or too swampy to grow crops. Today, Israel has blossomed into a world leader in agriculture technology.

Technology to Advance Agriculture

The actual amount of Israel's land used to grow crops is quite small, only 3.69 percent.[1] The agriculture industry itself only makes up 2.4 percent of Israel's GDP.[2] Only two percent of Israel's labor force works in agriculture.[3]

Despite these low percentages, Israeli farmers grow enough crops to feed the country's population. Most of the food eaten in Israel is produced in Israel. In addition, Israel exports over $2 billion in fresh produce to other countries each year.[4] Kibbutzim and agriculture companies have developed a range of agriculture technologies ("agritech") to overcome the small and inhospitable amount of land available to grow crops.

Israeli agriculture companies utilize technologies to:

- become the world's largest recycler of water. Israel recycles 80 percent of its wastewater.[5]
- reduce the volume of water needed to irrigate crops, allowing Israel to grow more crops while using less water. This method has also allowed Israel's overall water consumption to remain close to the rate in 1964, despite the fact its population has nearly quadrupled since then.[6]

- improve dairy production from animals. The average Israeli cow produces a third more milk each year than the typical American cow.[7]
- develop seeds and crops that can grow in dry, unfavorable conditions, as well as produce more plentiful crops
- raise fish in the desert without leaving environmentally dangerous waste behind

Israel's lack of natural resources and the need to be self-reliant were the motivation to create these technologies. The outcome is that Israel's largest agriculture business is really agritech. Israel's export of water technologies alone is already more than $2 billion a year,[8] and continues to increase rapidly. Overall, Israel agritech exports are in the range of $3.4 billion each year.[9] In the words of past President Shimon Peres, "Agriculture is 'ninety-five percent science, five percent work.'"[10]

Sharing with the World

Agri-technologies developed by Israeli kibbutzim and companies have been used to improve water use and crop yields in other food-challenged countries. To cite a few examples, Israeli agritech has been used to improve water supplies in China, increase crop productivity in India, reduce the need for chemical pesticides in California, and keep fruits and vegetables fresher for a longer period of time in Kenya.

Many countries face the challenge of a lack of reliable, edible food and potable water that Israel began to tackle decades ago. As a result, Israel's agritech exports are expected to grow in the future. In fact, some believe that Israel's agritech industry is still in its early stages. The idea is that the agritech sector should receive the same attention and investment as

Bulldozers crush tons of green wheat to turn it into fodder for dairy cows at the local animal feed center in the farming community of Beer Tuviya, southern Israel.

Dairy cows feed on fodder at a dairy farm in Kfar Haroeh, central Israel.

A worker screws lids on honey jars in a factory in Yad Mordechai, Israel.

An Israeli beekeeper is collecting honey in Kibbutz Yad Mordechai, Israel.

Growing organic food in Moshav Ein Tamar in the Judean Desert along the Dead Sea.

People shopping in Jerusalem's crowded Mahane Yehuda Market, which is filled with stalls of farm fresh food of all kinds, as well as many pastry, cheese, and coffee shops.

Israel's other technology sectors. The goal is to encourage increased innovation and at the same time make more agritech methods available on a global scale.

At present, Israel's water agritech industry is highly developed. Israeli companies provide solutions that make saltwater drinkable, improve the ability to recycle water, reduce the volume of water needed for crops, and help protect water resources. A variety of Israeli companies are also seeking ways to make crops grow on land where they haven't grown before and to produce more crops with less effort and use more environmentally-friendly farming methods.

Among the new areas being explored by Israeli agritech firms are:

- developing software to help farmers make better decisions about when and where to plant crops using crowd sourcing—a kind of social media approach to farming
- using "smart" robots capable of making decisions about which cows to milk and how much to feed a chicken
- creating "smart" farms that can send information about soil contents and conditions to farmers

The Israeli government is making a greater investment in agricultural research and development. The aim is to create "the Facebook of agriculture,"[11] a resource for agricultural research to be made available to farmers across the globe.

DRIP IRRIGATION

The Israeli company Netafim won the Stockholm Industry Water Award for 2013. The award is given to a company for its contribution to helping others use water better. Netafim achieves this goal with its drip irrigation technology.

Drip irrigation is the process of delivering just the right amount of water directly to a plant's roots. The watering tubes use friction to reduce the pressure as the water flows through the tubes. When water reaches the end of the tube, there's practically no water pressure at all.

Reducing the water pressure down the line means that water goes where it's needed, and doesn't rush to the end of the tube or evaporate. The benefit of watering crops through drip irrigation is that far less water is needed, yet more crops are grown.

This feat of engineering was created by a father and son team, Simcha (seem-CHA) and Yeshayahu (yeh-shah-YAH-hoo) Bass in 1959. Simcha was curious about a healthy tree he saw growing without any visible source of water. He investigated and found a leaky faucet that left a pool of water underground at the tree's roots. With this inspiration, he and his son eventually developed a drip irrigation technology they believed could help relieve Israel's water shortage.

However, Simcha knew that he needed investors in order to realize the potential of drip irrigation. Kibbutz Hatzerim (ha-tzeh-REEM) was enthusiastic about the prospects and bought the company in 1965. In the words of Naty Barak, the company's director of global responsibility, "We started drip irrigation not because we were smart, but because we had no choice."[12]

The kibbutz set up a company, Netafim, to develop the drip irrigation technology on a commercial basis. Today Netafim employs 3,000 people, but not only in Israel. It has 13 factories and 37 subsidiaries across 150 countries.[13]

Some highrise office buildings in Tel Aviv, Israel's largest city and financial center.

CHAPTER 5

NEW TECHNOLOGIES—
Israel at the Cutting Edge

Apple, Facebook, and Google wanted to buy this company. It had created an app that helps people avoid traffic. It was developed in Israel by a company with an annual revenue of less than $1 million in 2012.[1] In June 2013, Google made the acquisition. It bought the Israeli company called Waze for $966 million.[2] The Waze purchase was one of the larger purchases of Israeli tech companies in 2013. Foreign direct investment in Israel for all of 2013 was more than $11.5 billion, much of it made in Israel's technology sector.[3] Comparing to other OECD countries, foreigners invested the equivalent of 4 percent of Israel's GDP in Israel. The average foreign investment for an OECD country is just 1.5 percent.[4]

Starting Up and Digging In

Israel has more tech start-ups and companies than any location outside of the **Silicon Valley**, earning Israel the nickname the "Silicon Wadi." (wah-DEE, Arabic for "valley") **Tel Aviv** has been ranked as the world's second most hospitable city for start-ups, the only city outside of the United States to break into the top five.[5] While Israel's economy ranks high in overall competitiveness, its science and technology sector is ranked as the world's second most dynamic, just after South Korea.[6]

Buying and investing in Israel-based technology companies is just one way foreign companies show they value Israelis' creativity and productivity. Another way is by opening a research and development center (R&D) in Israel. Research and development centers are the places where companies explore and experiment with new technologies, products, and systems. They're the idea factories, where the companies try to find the next "big thing"—or at least a new way to stay competitive.

A company puts R&D centers where it thinks it can find the most creative and inventive workers. For many global technology giants, Israel is high on that list. Israel is home to roughly 250 R&D centers, including centers opened by Apple, Microsoft, Google, Facebook, Intel, IBM, Motorola, McAfee, Cisco, and Samsung. No country has a higher proportion of its labor force working in R&D than Israel.[7] For every 10,000 Israelis—140 work in R&D.[8] The United States has only 85 workers per 10,000 in R&D.[9] Israel spends more of its GDP on R&D than any other country as well—4.5 percent.[10]

So, Are They Coming Up with Anything Good?

Israeli companies, scientists, and engineers have been central to developing some of the world's most useful and interesting computer technologies for decades. Some of these Israeli innovations include:

- Intel's 8088 computer chip, the smallest chip designed in its time, which opened the way for computers to be small enough to be in an office or a home. Prior to the 8088 chip, computers were so big they took up entire rooms.

- Check Point developed the first commercially viable Internet security firewall product, the FW-1, which helped establish the foundation for ways to make the Internet safer.
- The world's first instant message (IM) program that allowed users on any computer running Microsoft Windows to IM one another. The name of the company was "ICQ" (say it out loud . . .) and it had over 50 million international users at its height. The company was eventually bought by AOL.
- M-Systems invented the USB flash drive, which has become the primary means of portable data storage, replacing the old methods, such as the CD-ROM and floppy disks.

And Those are Just Twentieth Century Innovations
In the twenty-first century, Israeli companies and R&D centers continue to produce key technologies: computer hardware, IT communications and security and applications. Some highlights, in addition to the Waze app are:

- Intel Israel designs and builds the Centrino microprocessor, the foundation for the development of modern, smaller, faster, wireless mobile devices.
- Project RAY has developed a smart phone that can be used by people with vision loss.
- PrimeSense, purchased by Apple, developed 3D sensors used in game devices as well as for medical devices and cars.

Keeping up with Israeli demand for cellphones is no easy task. This is a cellphone recycling plant in southern Israel. Pelephone, founded in 1986, was the first company to offer mobile phone services in Israel. Its name comes from the word "pele" (peh-leh), which means "wonder."

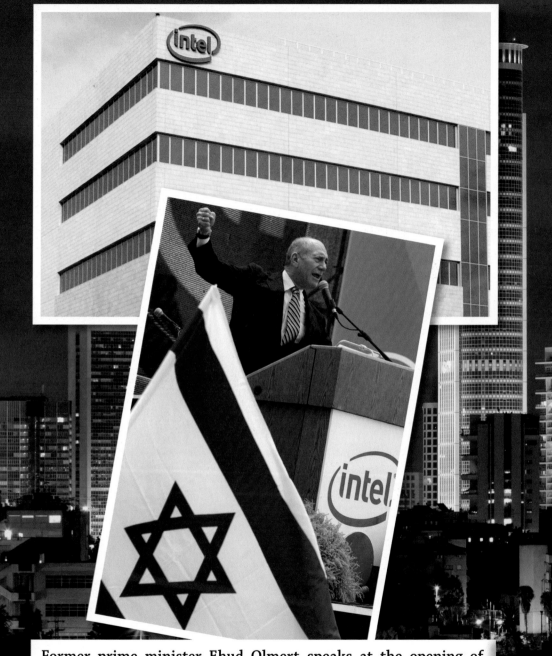

Former prime minister Ehud Olmert speaks at the opening of Intel's second plant in Kiryat Gat, a southern Israeli town. The first plant opened in 1999. The second plant, opened in 2008, is a high-volume manufacturing facility that produces products for all sizes of hardware, from servers to mobile devices.

- Glide, based in Jerusalem, developed a video text app for use on mobile phones.
- SlickLogin, purchased by Google when it was only two months old, has created a secure website login process using sound.

Computer and Internet innovations are just one aspect of Israel's technology sector. Agritech and environmental (also called "CleanTech") work is part of its technology sector as well. Israeli companies and R&D centers also make critical contributions to technology developments in medicine and medical devices, life sciences, defense, and space and satellite research.

Israeli company Urban Aeronautics LTD is developing an unmanned aerial vehicle called the AirMule. The model here shows the rotorless aircraft; an actual AirMule measures 20 feet long and over six feet wide. Testing of the first AirMule prototype began in 2014. Its size and lack of rotor or wings allows the AirMule to reach areas out of reach of a helicopter or airplane, like narrow urban streets or difficult natural terrain. The hope is that it can ferry supplies in and wounded soldiers out of dangerous areas more safely than is currently possible.

THE PILLCAM

Cameras aren't just for phones. Israeli inventor Gavriel Iddan used to work in an Israeli defense company where he focused on miniature optical devices to enable missiles to identify targets. The tiny optical devices inspired Iddan to think further. What if the technology that allowed these devices to be made so small could also be used to see other hard to reach places—like inside a patient's stomach?

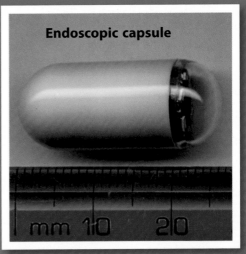

Endoscopic capsule

The result of Iddan's experimentation? The PillCam. The camera is so small it fits in a case no bigger than a pill—A pill that a patient can swallow, allowing the camera to take pictures as it travels through the intestines.

In order to work, the PillCam needed more than just a teeny-tiny video camera. Iddan also had to fit lights, batteries, and a wireless transmitter into the "pill." He had to make sure the PillCam would make a video clear enough to see and that it could transmit itself to a device outside the person's body. Iddan managed to fit all of that technology into a pill casing that was only 7/16th of an inch by 1 1/32 of an inch big, and weighed only 0.13 ounces.[11]

Iddan co-founded his company, Given Imaging, in 1998. Since then, the company's PillCams have been used more than 2 million times, allowing doctors to achieve early detection of diseases in the digestive system.[12] Before the PillCam, the only way doctors could see directly into the intestines was through potentially dangerous, painful, and costly surgery. With the PillCam, doctors have a safer, more comfortable way to help patients.

Endoscopic capsule showing six LEDs and camera lens

One of Tel Aviv's electric power stations, lit up at night and powering Israel's largest city

Let There Be Light . . . and Natural Gas

Israelis have long joked about how odd it is that Israel is the "Promised Land" when it is the only region in the Middle East without any oil. The jokes stopped in 2009. Israelis didn't find oil. But huge reserves of natural gas were enough to make Israel an exporter of energy—after it meets its own energy needs.

However, prior to 2009, Israel's energy sector was similar to so many other Israeli industries. It suffered from a lack of natural energy resources and an abundance of high security risks. The country was only able to produce small amounts of petroleum, coal, and natural gas. Even the available natural resources required assistance from other countries to transform them into usable energy. Oil had long been Israel's primary energy source, and nearly all of it had to be imported.

Israel faced two great risks to its energy supply. The first was that foreign sources would stop their flow of supplies into Israel. Since most oil reserves were found in countries hostile to Israel, many international energy sector companies didn't want to work with Israel for fear of making the oil-producing countries angry. Israel's second major energy risk was an attack on one of its few oil refineries, which would greatly damage the country's ability to defend itself from a larger attack.

Since the State's earliest days, Israel searched for alternatives. As one scholar describes it, "Few countries had looked so hard with so few results."[1] This situation forced Israelis to be as creative as they could. Israel might not have typical Middle Eastern oil reserves, but it does have typical Middle Eastern sunshine. Israel went through a serious fuel shortage in the 1950s. In response, an Israeli engineer, Levi Yasser, started Israel's first solar heating company. The company built solar water heaters. In 1967, five percent of Israeli homes were already using the solar heaters to heat their water.[2] Today, solar water heaters sit atop 90 percent of Israel's apartment buildings and homes.[3] However, Israel has remained dangerously dependent on other countries to meet its energy needs.

Solar water heaters on a roof

Searching for Energy Independence

In 2010, the Israeli government announced its intention to have alternative energy provide 10 percent of its electricity by 2020.[4] A number of companies have already begun building solar panel farms in Israel's large Negev Desert, making Israel the country with the fastest growing solar panel market in the world by 2009.[5] Progress in research and development in Israel's solar industry attracted investment from both foreign companies and governments.

Critics say that despite the country's development of key solar technologies used around the world and building multiple solar panel farms in the south, Israel hasn't yet made practical use of solar power beyond the solar water heaters. Estimates are that solar power only accounts for a small percentage of Israel's total energy usage. The critics blame government inaction and unpredictable regulation.

A New Energy Industry

Critics of Israel's limited solar power use also fear that the recently discovered large natural gas deposits are diverting the Israeli government's attention away from solar power. The size of the natural gas deposits are diverting indeed.

The Tamar deposit, discovered in 2009, is believed to hold an estimated 8.5 trillion cubic feet of natural gas. This find was overshadowed the following year, when another deposit, believed to hold an estimated 16-18 trillion cubic feet of natural gas, was discovered. This deposit was named "Leviathan." Both natural gas reserves are in the Mediterranean Sea, between 50 and 80 miles west of the northern city of **Haifa**. Israel began extracting natural gas from the Tamar reserve in March 2013 and expects to start attaining natural gas from the Leviathan reserve by 2016.

Extracting the natural gas from these deposits, transporting it and making it into usable energy involves a variety of companies from many different countries. In fact, the discoveries themselves were made by a Texas company that bought the license to explore the area from an Israeli company. It's estimated that another $40 billion in investments in Israel's natural gas sector will be required by 2020.[6]

The natural gas finds will also have great impact on the Israeli economy and workforce. Israel could save millions of dollars in energy purchases every month. The cost of energy to Israelis would be lower, allowing some large-scale enterprises,

Israeli oil refinery in Haifa, Israel

A gas rig in the Tamar natural gas field is guarded by the Israeli navy. The field reached its full production capacity in July 2013. There are five underwater wells that all feed into the Tamar platform.

Orot Rabin, located in the north of the country, is Israel's largest power station.

Israel has three major ports, Haifa in the north, Eilat in the south, and this one: The Port of Ashdod, just south of Tel Aviv in the middle of the country's Mediterranean coast.

previously impractical, to become economically viable. Indeed, some have suggested that the lower energy costs would allow Israel to expand its water desalination plants, which require a great deal of energy to operate. This may lead Israel to become an exporter of water as well as gas.[7]

A recent report showed that production from the Tamar reserve increased Israel's GDP growth by nearly a half a percent in 2013, and projected it would add another 1.5 percent to the nation's GDP in 2014.[8] The Bank of Israel expects that the country's currency will also grow stronger as the country spends less money on importing oil.[9]

The need for skilled workers in areas such as deep sea drilling, pipeline construction, and other energy-related services, will be in high demand. However, it is not yet clear whether Israel will develop a domestic workforce with these skills, or if the foreign companies highly invested in Israel's natural gas reserves will import the labor.

As it stands today, Israel is a first world economy with high energy demands. The security risks linked to energy have not changed, even if Israel's access to natural resources has. There are a number of open questions with regard to Israel's ability to make the most of its domestic solar and natural gas resources. This means that maintaining access to energy still poses a risk to Israel's economy and security.

Of course, risk is nothing new to Israel or its people. From the start of the modern Zionist movement in the nineteenth century and until today, Israelis have responded to the risks around them with resourcefulness, creativity and daring. These values strengthened them as they met the challenge of re-establishing Israel in its ancient homeland. Now, in the twenty-first century, these values will help them create economic opportunity for all Israelis and bring innovation to the world.

ENERGY AS A RESOURCE TO ADVANCE PEACE

Israel and Jordan came to an agreement by which Israel will supply Jordan with $500 million worth of natural gas from the Tamar reserve over 15 years, starting in 2016.[10] The deal also leaves room for the two former enemies to create a partnership valued at $30 billion, which would position Israel as Jordan's main supplier of gas. This partnership was born of a shared interest between the two countries— unreliable access to Egypt's gas in the wake of the **Arab Spring**. The deal with Jordan does not represent the first time Israel has demonstrated its willingness to use energy resources to promote peace. As natural gas reserves were found off Israel's coast, another reserve was also found off the Gaza coast in waters that span areas of control of both Israel and the **Palestinian Authority** (PA). The find is believed large enough to meet the energy needs of Palestinians, as well as provide the basis for at least some export. Most of this reserve is in PA waters, and Israel agreed to have the boundary line redrawn so the entire find would be within PA waters.[11]

Israel made a similar move decades ago with Egypt. For a short time in the 1970s, it also seemed likely that Israel might gain energy independence. It had captured the **Sinai Peninsula** from Egypt during the Six-Day War in 1967. The Sinai had enough oil fields to make Israel self-sufficient. These oil fields provided Israel with considerable strategic and security value. However, Israel agreed to return the Sinai Peninsula, along with ownership of its oil fields, to Egypt as part of the historic 1979 Egypt-Israel Peace Treaty.

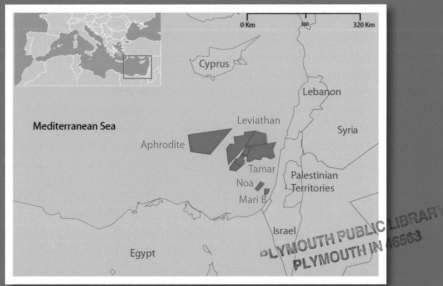

Major Gas Fields in the Eastern Mediterranean Sea

TIMELINE

1909	Kibbutz Degania, the first kibbutz, is established.
1920	HaHistradrut, Israel's largest trade union, is formed.
1948	Israel declares its independence as a sovereign state on May 14.
1952	IDF Unit 8200 is created.
1954	Bank of Israel is established.
1966	Netafim sells its first drip irrigation equipment to an Israeli vineyard.
1967	Six Day War between Israel and Egypt, Jordan, and Syria, fought from June 5–10.
1973	Yom Kippur War between Israel and Egypt, Syria, and a variety of other Muslim states.
1977	Talpiot Unit created in IDF, the idea for unit resulting from failures during the Yom Kippur War; the Likud party wins election, the first time in Israel's history that a non-left wing aligned party had won.
1979	Israel signs peace with Egypt and returns the Sinai Peninsula and its oil fields to Egypt as part of the agreement; Intel introduces the 8088 computer chip, designed and developed in its Israeli R&D center.
1984	Inflation in Israel averages 450 percent.
1985	Israeli government provides kibbutzim with massive financial bailout as part of its Stabilization Plan of 1985, intended to fix the country's major economic problems; Israel signs free trade agreement with the United States.
1998	AOL buys Israeli company that developed ICQ, the world's most popular Internet chat program at the time, for $287 million.
1991	Microsoft opens strategic R&D center in Israel.
1994	Israel and Jordan sign peace accord.
1999	Israeli inventor Shimon Shmueli invents the USB flash drive.
2003	Intel's Israeli R&D team design and develop the Centrino microprocessor. Benjamin Netanyahu appointed Finance Minister, where he served until 2005; he implements series of financial reforms to lower government spending and make Israeli economy more competitive.
2006	Google opens its first R&D center in the Middle East in Israel.
2008	Israel's GDP starts dropping in late 2008 as the world goes through recession, but starts showing positive growth by mid-2009.
2009	Tamar Natural gas field found off the coast of Israel.
2010	Israel joins the Organization for Economic Cooperation and Development (OECD); Leviathan natural gas field found off the Israeli coast.
2013	Google buys Israeli app developer Waze for $966 million.
2014	Israeli company Soda Stream airs a commercial during the Super Bowl; Israel and Jordan sign a $500 million agreement for Israel to provide natural gas to Jordan.
2015	Israeli startup companies sold for a record $860 million in January alone, nearly 50 percent more than the 2014 monthly average of $578 million. Apple opens its second largest R&D center in the world in Herzliya, Israel

CHAPTER NOTES

Introduction

1. "Economic Highlights 2nd Quarter 2014," Israel Finance Ministry, http://www.financeisrael.mof.gov.il/FinanceIsrael/Docs/En/EconomicHighlights/EconomicHighlightsPresentation-2014-2.pdf
2. "Social Networking Statistics," July 9, 2014, Statistics Brain, http://www.statisticbrain.com/social-networking-statistics
3. Dan Senor and Saul Singer, *Start-Up Nation* (New York: Twelve, 2009), p. 8.
4. "Bank Hapoalim's CEO Inaugurated the Bank's new index trading floors," January 21, 2014, BankHapoalim, http://www.bankhapoalim.com/wps/portal/int/article?WCM_GLOBAL_CONTEXT=/wps/wcm/connect/bhint/int/home/irelations/pressreleasessa/inauguratdthebanksnewtradingfloors&proceed=1
5. "Israeli Society & Culture: The Histradrut." Jewish Virtual Library, http://www.jewishvirtuallibrary.org/jsource/History/histadrut.html
6. Senor and Singer, *Start-up Nation*, p. xi.

Chapter 1: More than Sheer Daring: The Enduring Values of the Kibbutz

1. Joshua Muravchik, *Heaven on Earth The Rise and Fall of Socialism* (San Francisco: Encounter Books, 2002), p. 333.
2. Kibbutz Program Center. "About Kibbutz" http://www.kibbutzprogramcenter.org/about-kibbutz
3. Keshet Rosenblum, "Living out their ideals on an eight-floor urban kibbutz," *Haaretz*, December 25, 2013, http://www.haaretz.com/news/features/.premium-1.565060
4. Kibbutz Program Center. "About Kibbutz" http://www.kibbutzprogramcenter.org/about-kibbutz

Chapter 2: Israel's Workforce: The Challenge of Opening the Door to Fuller Employment

1. "Labour Force Survey Data, November 2013," Israel Central Bureau of Statistics.
2. "Israel," OECD Better Life Index. http://www.oecdbetterlifeindex.org/countries/israel/
3. "Israel," OECD Better Life Index.
4. Niv Elis, "Flug warns demographic trends could cost Israel 1.3% of annual growth rate," *The Jerusalem Post*, February 18, 2014, p. 6.
5. "Israel 2013," OECD Economic Surveys, p. 6.
6. "Israel Business Forecast Report Q1 2014," Business Monitor International, p. 5.
7. "Education at a Glance 2013 Israel," OECD, p. 1.
8. Ibid.
9. "Israel," OECD Better Life Index.
10. "Labor Force Survey Data, November 2013," Israel Central Bureau of Statistics.
11. Ibid.
12. "Education at a Glance 2013 Israel," OECD, p 3.
13. "Israel December 2013," OECD Economic Surveys, p. 2.
14. "Flug calls for more Arabs, haredim in workforce," *Globes,* October 29, 2013.
15. Elis, "Flug warns demographic trends could cost Israel 1.3% of annual growth rate."
16. "Recent Economic Developments," Bank of Israel, December 2, 2013.
17. Lior Dattel, "Tax data: Half of all Israelis earn under NIS 5,812 a month," *Haaretz*, July 25, 2012, http://www.haaretz.com/business/tax-data-half-of-all-israelis-earn-under-nis-5-812-a-month-1.453451
18. Haim Bior, "One in eight Israelis paid less than minimum wage," *Haaretz*, August 19, 2013, http://www.haaretz.com/news/national/.premium-1.542225
19. Bior, "One in eight Israelis paid less than minimum wage."

Chapter 3: Mandatory Service in the IDF: The Army Means Business in Israel

1. Senor and Singer, *Start-up Nation*, p. 48. The entire story about this soldier is from this book.
2. Senor and Singer, *Start-up Nation*, p. 25.
3. "Unit 8200 and Israel's high-tech whiz kids," UPI, June 4, 2012, http://www.upi.com/Business_News/SecurityIndustry/2012/06/04/Unit-8200-and-Israels-high-tech-whiz-kids/UPI-43661338833765/
4. UPI, "Unit 8200 and Israel's high-tech whiz kids."
5. Senor and Singer, *Start-up Nation*, p. 70.
6. Ibid.
7. Abigail Klein Leichman, "The IDF incubator for Israel's future CEOs," Israel21c, September 19, 2012, http://israel21c.org/technology/the-idf-incubator-for-israels-future-ceos/
8. Klein Leichman, "The IDF incubator for Israel's future CEOs."
9. Ibid.

10. "Reform of Exemption Law Boding Well for Economy," Business Monitor Online, March 3, 2014.

Chapter 4: Making the Desert Bloom

1. "Israel," CIA World Factbook, https://www.cia.gov/library/publications/the-worldfactbook/geos/is.html
2. "Israel," CIA World Factbook.
3. Ibid.
4. Abigail Klein Leichman, "Top 12 new fruit and vegetable species developed in Israel," Israel21c, May 28, 2013, http://israel21c.org/environment/top-12-new-fruit-and-vegetables-species-developed-in-israel/
5. Sharon Udasin, "'Israel has room for in-home water recycling,'" *The Jerusalem Post*, October 21, 2012,http://www.jpost.com/Enviro-Tech/Israel-has-room-for-in-home-water-recycling
6. William Booth, "Israel knows water technology, and it wants to cash in," *The Washington Post*, http://www.washingtonpost.com/world/middle_east/israel-knows-water-technology-and-it-wants-to-cashin/2013/10/25/bb1dd36-3cc5-11e3-b0e7-716179a2c2c7_story.html
7. Yuk Lun Chan, "How Israel Became The World Leader in Milking Technologies," No Camels, March 17, 2013, http://nocamels.com/2013/03/how-israel-became-the-world-leader-in-milking-technologies/
8. Yuval Azulai and Tzahi Hoffman, "Israeli water tech exports top $2b annually," Globes, October 22, 2013, http://www.globes.co.il/en/article-1000887770
9. "Israeli agritech firm promising growth in crop yields," Reuters, November 15, 2013, http://www.reuters.com/article/2013/11/15/agritech-israel-idUSL5N0Il2TA20131115
10. Senor and Singer, *Start-up Nation*, p. 226.
11. Sharon Udasin, "VC firm chief says agritech can be Israel's next 'hi-tech,'" *The Jerusalem Post*, December 4, 2013.,http://www.jpost.com/Enviro-Tech/VC-firm-chief-says-agritech-can-be-Israels-next-hi-tech-333906
12. Jeffrey Marlow. "Business Booming at Drip-Irrigation Company," *The New York Times*, September 17, 2009, http://green.blogs.nytimes.com/2009/09/17/business-booming-for-drip-irrigation-firm/?_php=true&_type=blogs&_r=0

13. David Shamah, "What Israeli drips did for the world," *The Times of Israel*, August 20, 2013, http://www.timesofisrael.com/what-israeli-drips-did-for-the-world/

Chapter 5: New Technologies: Israel at the Cutting Edge

1. Timothy Stenovec, "Google Buys Waze: Social Mapping App Will 'Enhance' Google Maps," *The Huffington Post*, June 1, 2013, http://www.huffingtonpost.com/2013/06/11/google-buys-waze-social-mapping-app_n_3422097.html
2. Dara Kerr, "Google reveals it spent $966 million in Waze acquisition," *CNet*, July 25, 2013, http://news.cnet.com/83011023_3-57595620-93/google-reveals-it-spent-$966-million-in-waze-acquisition/
3. "Leumi Economic Weekly," Bank Leumi, January 8, 2014.
4. Ibid.
5. Rip Empson, "Startup Genome Ranks The World's Startup Ecosystems: Silicon Valley, Tel Aviv & L.A. Lead the Way," TechCrunch.com, November 20, 2012, http://techcrunch.com/2012/11/20/startup-genome-ranks-the-worlds-topstartup-ecosystems-silicon-valley-tel-aviv-l-a-lead-the-way/
6. Zach Pontz, "Israel Ranks Second on Global Dynamism Index Science and Technology Sector," *The Algemeiner*, November 7, 2013, http://www.algemeiner.com/2013/11/17/israel-ranks-second-on-global-dynamism-index-science-and-technology-sector/
7. Yoram Ettinger, "Israeli economy defies economic meltdown at 65," JNS.org News Service, April 21, 2013, http://www.jns.org/latest-articles/2013/4/21/at-65-israel-defies-economic-meltdown#.UxR-mNxRfwl
8. Ibid.
9. Ibid.
10. Ibid.
11. "Making gastrointestinal diagnostics easier to digest," European Patent Office, http://www.epo.org/learningevents/european-inventor/finalists/2011/iddan.html
12. Joshua Levitt, "US FDA Approves Use of Latest Israeli Invented PillCam to Monitor Crohn's Disease," *The Algemeiner*, August 13, 2013, http://www.algemeiner.com/2013/08/13/us-fda-approves-use-of-latest-israeli-invented-pillcam-tomonitor-crohns-disease/

CHAPTER NOTES

Chapter 6: Let There Be Light . . . and Natural Gas

1. Bahgat, Gawdat, "Israel's Energy Security: Regional Implications," *Middle East Policy Council*, Fall 2011, vol. XVIII, no. 3, http://www.mepc.org/journal/middle-east-policy-archives/israels-energy-security-regional-implications
2. Alexander Vagg. "Here Comes the Sun: Israel and Solar Energy," *Breaking Energy*, February 22, 2013, http://breakingenergy.com/2013/02/22/here-comes-the-sun-israel-and-solar-energy/
3. Vagg, "Here Comes the Sun: Israel and Solar Energy."
4. "Israel focuses its energy on clean technologies," Associated Press, January 5, 2011, http://www.jpost.com/EnviroTech/Israel-focuses-its-energy-on-clean-technologies
5. Itay Zetelny, "Renewable Energy Recap: Israel," RenewableEnergyWorld.com, January 2, 2012, http://www.renewableenergyworld.com/rea/news/article/2012/01/renewable-energy-recap-israel
6. "Overview of the Oil & Gas Industry in Israel," The Federation of Israeli Chambers of Commerce, March 2013, http://www.chamber.org.il/images/Files/21775/Overview.pdf
7. David Wurmser, "The Geopolitics of Israel's Offshore Gas Reserves," Jerusalem Center for Public Affairs, April 4, 2013, http://jcpa.org/article/the-geopolitics-of-israels-offshore-gas-reserves/
8. Amiram Barkat, "E&Y: Tamar gas worth $52b to Israel," *Globes*, January 7, 2014, http://www.globes.co.il/en/article1000907759
9. Barkat, "E&Y: Tamar gas worth $52b to Israel."
10. "Israel-Jordan sign $500 million natural gas deal," *The Times of Israel*, February 19, 2014, http://www.timesofisrael.com/israel-jordan-sign-500-million-natural-gas-deal/
11. Wurmser, "The Geopolitics of Israel's Offshore Gas Reserves."

WORKS CONSULTED

Allouche, David. "Israeli Technology Allows Growing Fish In The Desert." *No Camels*. April 22, 2012. http://nocamels.com/2012/04/israeli-technology-allows-growing-fish-in-the-desert/

Associated Press. "Israel focuses its energy on clean technologies." *The Jerusalem Post*. January 5, 2011. http://www.jpost.com/Enviro-Tech/Israel-focuses-its-energy-on-clean-technologies

Azulai, Yuval and Tzahi Hoffman. "Israeli water tech exports top $2b annually." *Globes*. October 22, 2013. http://www.globes.co.il/en/article-1000887770

Bahgat, Gawdat. "Israel's Energy Security: Regional Implications." Middle East Policy Council, Fall 2011 Vol. XVIII, no. 3. http://www.mepc.org/journal/middle-east-policy-archives/israels-energy-security-regional-implications?print

Bank Hapoalim. "Bank Hapoalim's CEO Inaugurated the Bank's new index trading floors." January 21, 2014. http://www.bankhapoalim.com/wps/portal/int/articleWCM_GLOBAL_CONTEXT=/wps/wcm/connect/bhint/inthome/irelations/pressreleasessa/inauguratedthebanksnewtradingfloors&proceed=1

Bank Leumi. "Leumi Economic Weekly." January 8, 2014.

Bank of Israel. "Recent Economic Developments." December 2, 2013.

Barkat, Amiram. "'Solar power is Israel's only alternative." *Globes*. October 7, 2013. http://www.globes.co.il/en/article-1000861261

———. "Israel must build energy services industry." *Globes*. February, 9, 2014. http://www.globes.co.il/en/article-israel-must-build-energy-services-industry-1000915890

Barkat, Amiram. "E&Y: Tamar gas worth $52b to Israel." *Globes*. January 7, 2014. http://www.globes.co.il/article-1000907759

Bior, Haim. "One in eight Israelis paid less than minimum wage." *Haaretz*. August 19, 2013. http://www.haaretz.com/news/national/.premium-1.542225

Business Monitor International. "Israel Business Forecast Report Q1 2014."

Business Monitor Online. "Reform of Exemption Law Boding Well for Economy." March 3, 2014.

Booth, William. "Israel knows water technology, and it wants to cash in." *The Washington Post*. October 25, 2013. http://www.washingtonpost.com/world/middle_east/israel-knows-water-technology-and-it-wants-to-cash-in/2013/10/25/7bb1dd36-3cc5-11e3-b0e7-716179a2c2c7_story.html

CIA World Factbook: "Israel." https://www.cia.gov/library/publications/the-world-factbook/geos/is.html

Dattel, Lior. "Tax data: Half of all Israelis earn under NIS 5,812 a month." *Haaretz*. July 25, 2012. http://www.haaretz.com/business/tax-data-half-of-all-israelis-earn-under-nis-5-812-a-month-1.453451

Economic History Association. "A Brief Economic History of Modern Israel." http://eh.net/encyclopedia/a-brief-economic-history-of-modern-israel/

WORKS CONSULTED

Einat Paz-Frankel. "Exit Nation: Israeli Startups Sell for $860 Million in First Four Weeks of 2015," NoCamels.com. January 31, 2015. http://nocamels. com/2015/01/israeli-startups-acquired-by-amazon-and-dropbox/

Elis, Niv. "Flug warns demographic trends could cost Israel 1.3% of annual growth rate." *The Jerusalem Post*. February 18, 2014.

Empson, Rip. "Startup Genome Ranks The World's Startup Ecosystems: Silicon Valley, Tel Aviv & L.A. Lead the Way." TechCrunch.com. November 20, 2012. http://techcrunch.com/2012/11/20/ startup-genome-ranks-the-worlds-top-startup-ecosystems-silicon-valley-tel-aviv-l-a-lead-the-way/

Ettinger, Yoram. "Israeli economy defies economic meltdown at 65." JNS.org News Service. April 21, 2013. http://www.jns.org/latest-articles/2013/4/21/at-65-israel-defies-economic-meltdown#.UxR-mNxRfwI

European Patent Office. "Making gastrointestinal diagnostics easier to digest." http://www.epo.org/ learning-events/european-inventor/finalists/2011/ iddan.html

The Federation of Israeli Chambers of Commerce. "Overview of the Oil & Gas Industry in Israel." March 2013. http://www.chamber.org.il/images/ Files/21775/Overview.pdf

"Flug calls for more Arabs, haredim in workforce." *Globes*. October 29, 2013.

Harkov, Lahav. "Edelstein: Haredi conscription bill could tear nation apart." *The Jerusalem Post*. March 2, 2014. http://www.jpost.com/Diplomacy-and-Politics/Edelstein-Haredi-conscription-bill-could-bring-civil-war-344020

International Monetary Fund. "Israel 2013 Article IV Consultation." IMF Country Report No. 14/47.

Israel Central Bureau of Statistics. "Labor Force Survey Data, November 2013."

Israel Ministry of Finance. "Economic Highlights," citing OECD (2011) and World Economic Forum (2013-2014) statistics.

Israel Ministry of Foreign Affairs. "Israel in Brief." http://mfa.gov.il/MFA/AboutIsrael/Pages/ ISRAEL%20IN%20BRIEF.aspx

Israel Ministry of Industry, Trade & Labor. "Foreign R&D Centers in Israel." August 2011.

Jewish Virtual Library. "Israeli Society & Culture: The Histradrut." http://www.jewishvirtuallibrary.org/ jsource/History/histadrut.html

Johnson, George. "Scholars Debate Roots of Yiddish, Migration of Jews." *New York Times*. October 29, 1996. http://www.nytimes.com/1996/10/29/ science/scholars-debate-roots-of-yiddish-migration-of-jews.html

Johnson, Rachel. "The kibbutz goes capitalist." *The Spectator*. April 6, 2013. http://www.spectator.co. uk/features/8880121/the-end-of-a-kibbutz-dream/

Kam, Laura. "Israel helps stem global food crisis." YNetnews.com, August 4, 2011. http://www. ynetnews.com/articles/0,7340,L-4097075,00.html

KenIvest. "With Israeli tech, Amiran Kenya looks to boost East Africa's farmers." February 19, 2014. http://www.investmentkenya.com/latest-news/442- with-israeli-tech-amiran-kenya-looks-to-boost-east-africa-s-farmers

Kerr, Dara. "Google reveals it spent $966 million in Waze acquisition." CNet.com. July 25, 2013. http://news.cnet.com/8301-1023_3-57595620- 93/google-reveals-it-spent-$966-million-in-waze-acquisition/

Klein Leichman, Abigail. "The top 12 ways Israel feeds the world," Israel21c.com. May 10, 2012. http:// israel21c.org/technology/the-top-12-ways-israel-feeds-the-world/

Klein Leichman, Abigail. "The IDF incubator for Israel's future CEOs," Israel21c.com. September 19, 2012. http://israel21c.org/technology/ the-idf-incubator-for-israels-future-ceos/

Klein Leichman, Abigail. "Top 12 new fruit and vegetable species developed in Israel." Israel21c. com. May 28, 2013. http://israel21c.org/ environment/top-12-new-fruit-and-vegetables-species-developed-in-israel/

Kloosterman, Karin. "The Waze of agriculture." Israel21c.com, January 29, 2014. http://israel21c. org/headlines/the-waze-of-agriculture/

Levitt, Joshua. "US FDA Approves Use of Latest Israeli Invented PillCam to Monitor Crohn's Disease." *The Algemeiner*. August 13, 2013. http://www. algemeiner.com/2013/08/13/us-fda-approves-use-of-latest-israeli-invented-pillcam-to-monitor-crohns-disease/

Yuk Lun Chan. "How Israel Became The World Leader in Milking Technologies." NoCamels.com. March 17, 2013. http://nocamels.com/2013/03/ how-israel-became-the-world-leader-in-milking-technologies/

Mayor, Tracy. "CIO 20/20 Honorees - Innovator's Profile: Gil Schwed of Check Point Software Technologies, Ltd." *CIO Magazine*, October 1, 2002. http://www.cio.com/article/31405/ CIO_20_20_Honorees_Innovator_s_Profile_Gil_ Schwed_of_Check_Point_Software_Technologies_ Ltd.

Maleval, Jean-Jacques. "Who Invented the USB Flash Drive?" Storagenewsletter.com. February 13, 2013. http://www.storagenewsletter.com/rubriques/ solid-state-ssd-flash-key/who-invented-usb-flash-drive/

Marlow, Jeffrey. "Business Booming at Drip-Irrigation Company." *The New York Times*. September 17, 2009. http://green.blogs.nytimes. com/2009/09/17/business-booming-for-drip-irrigation-firm/?_php=true&_type=blogs&_r=0

McCarthy, Rory. "Israel's oldest kibbutz votes for privatization." *The Guardian*. February 20, 2007. http://www.theguardian.com/world/2007/feb/20/ israel1

Muravchik, Joshua. *Heaven on Earth The Rise and Fall of Socialism*. San Francisco: Encounter Books, 2002.

WORKS CONSULTED

Netafim. http://www.netafimlegacy.com/timeline

OECD Better Life Index. "Israel" http://www.oecdbetterlifeindex.org/countries/israel/

OECD Economic Surveys. "Israel 2013."

OECD. "Education at a Glance 2013 Israel."

Orpaz, Inbal. "R&D culture: Israeli enterprise, Chinese harmony." *Haaretz*. January 7, 2014. http://www.haaretz.com/business/1.567238

Petroff, Alanna. "Big tech scrambles for Israeli firms." CNN. November 22, 2013. http://money.cnn.com/2013/11/22/technology/israel-tech-boom/

Pontz, Zach. "Israel Ranks Second on Global Dynamism Index Science and Technology Sector." *The Algemeiner*. November 7, 2013. http://www.algemeiner.com/2013/11/17/israel-ranks-second-on-global-dynamism-index-science-and-technology-sector/

Reuters. "Israeli agritech firm promising growth in crop yields." November 15, 2013. http://www.reuters.com/article/2013/11/15/agritech-israel-idUSL5N0II2TA20131115

Rosenblum, Keshet. "Living out their ideals on an eight-floor urban kibbutz." *Haaretz*. December 25, 2013. http://www.haaretz.com/news/features/.premium-1.565060

Scheer, Steven. "Israeli gas group in talks on pipelines to Turkey, Jordan, Egypt." *Reuters*. August 6, 2013. http://www.reuters.com/article/2013/08/06/delek-natgas-exports-idUSL6N0G72F920130806

Senor, Dan and Saul Singer. *Start-Up Nation The Story of Israel's Economic Miracle*. New York: Twelve, 2011.

Shamah, David. "As demand for food rises, Israel doubles up on agritech." *The Times of Israel*. November 7, 2012. http://www.timesofisrael.com/as-demand-for-food-doubles-israel-doubles-up-on-agritech/

Shamah, David. "What Israeli drips did for the world." *The Times of Israel*. August 20, 2013. http://www.timesofisrael.com/what-israeli-drips-did-for-the-world/

Sherwood, Harriet. "Israel's kibbutz movement makes a comeback." *The Guardian*. July 23, 2012. http://www.theguardian.com/world/2012/jul/23/israel-kibbutz-movement-comeback

Shpancer, Noam. "Child of the collective." *The Guardian*. February 19, 2011. http://www.theguardian.com/lifeandstyle/2011/feb/19/kibbutz-child-noam-shpancer

Sobczak, Blake. "Israel's solar power struggles against government." *Bloomberg Business Week*. August 28, 2012. http://www.businessweek.com/ap/2012-08-28/israels-solar-power-struggles-against-government#p1

Statistics Brain. "Social Networking Statistics." http://www.statisticbrain.com/social-networking-statistics/

Times of Israel. "Israel-Jordan sign $500 million natural gas deal." February 19, 2014. http://www.timesofisrael.com/israel-jordan-sign-500-million-natural-gas-deal/

Timothy Stenovec. "Google Buys Waze: Social Mapping App Will 'Enhance' Google Maps." *The Huffington Post*. June 11, 2013. http://www.huffingtonpost.com/2013/06/11/google-buys-waze-social-mapping-app_n_3422097.html

Washington Times. "Kibbutz ideal collapses as Israel shifts to capitalism." March 4, 2007. http://www.washingtontimes.com/news/2007/mar/4/20070304-114147-6135r/?page=all

Wurmser, David. "The Geopolitics of Israel's Offshore Gas Reserves." Jerusalem Center for Public Affairs. April 4, 2013. http://jcpa.org/article/the-geopolitics-of-israels-offshore-gas-reserves/

Udasin, Sharon. "VC firm chief says agritech can be Israel's next 'hi-tech.'" *The Jerusalem Post*, December 4, 2013. http://www.jpost.com/Enviro-Tech/VC-firm-chief-says-agritech-can-be-Israels-next-hi-tech-333906

Udasin, Sharon. "Israel has room for in-home water recycling." *The Jerusalem Post*. October 21, 2012. http://www.jpost.com/Enviro-Tech/Israel-has-room-for-in-home-water-recycling

UPI. "Unit 8200 and Israel's high-tech whiz kids." June 4, 2012. http://www.upi.com/Business_News/Security-Industry/2012/06/04/Unit-8200-and-Israels-high-tech-whiz-kids/UPI-43661338833765/

Vagg, Alexander. "Here Comes the Sun: Israel and Solar Energy." Breaking Energy. February 22, 2013. http://breakingenergy.com/2013/02/22/here-comes-the-sun-israel-and-solar-energy/

Zetelny, Itay. "Renewable Energy Recap: Israel." RenewableEnergyWorld.com, January 2, 2012. http://www.renewableenergyworld.com/rea/news/article/2012/01/renewable-energy-recap-israel

Further Reading

Challoner, Jack. *DK Eyewitness Books: Energy*, New York: DK Children, 2012.

Hess, Karl. *Capitalism for Kids*, Placerville, California: Bluestocking PR, 2005.

Raum, Elizabeth. *The History of Computers*, Portsmouth, New Hampshire: Heinemann, 2007.

Walden-Kaplan, Kathy. *The Dog of Knots*, Reston, Virginia: MAB Books, 2012. (novel about a 9-year- old Israeli girl during the Yom Kippur War)

On the Internet

Economy of Israel
http://encyclopedia.kids.net.au/page/ec/Economy_of_Israel

Kid's Economic Glossary
http://www.scholastic.com/browse/article.jsp?id=3750579

USA Today:"List of Israel's Natural Resources"
http://traveltips.usatoday.com/list-israels-natural-resources-63037.html

Israel 21c: "Top 10 Israeli Apps for Kids"
http://www.israel21c.org/technology/top-10-israeli-apps-for-kids/

GLOSSARY

algorithm (EL-go-ri-thm)—a set of instructions to conduct calculations or reasoning to determine an outcome

Arab Spring—refers to series of revolutions in Arab countries that began in late 2010; many of the revolutions remain unsettled

audacious (aw-DAY-shuss)—willingness to take risks; highly original or creative

Bedouin (beh-doe-WIN)—once nomadic tribes who live in Israel's Negev Desert and other regions of the central Middle East

Capitalist (KEH-pih-tull-ist)—an economic theory based on free-market and individual ownership of property and labor with little government involvement

Druze (drooz)—a monotheistic religious and social community which keeps its beliefs and practices private. A small proportion of the Druze community lives in Israel and larger communities are found in Syria, Lebanon and Jordan

entrepreneur (ahn-trih-PA-noor)—an individual who takes the initiative—and risk—of starting a business..

Gaza (GAH-zuh)—also called the Gaza Strip, a strip of land between southwest Israel and the Mediterranean Sea which is under Palestinian control

Gross Domestic Product (GDP) (grow-ss doh-MEH-stick prah-DUCT)—total value of all the goods and services produced in a country. Its rate of growth or decline, measured as a percentage, is used to mark the economic health of a country

hyperinflation (high-PURR in-flay-SHUN)—"inflation" is an economic term to describe when money becomes less valuable, that is the same amount of money can't buy as much as it did in the past; hyperinflation is the steep and swift reduction in the value of money

Kinneret (key-near-EHT)—a large lake in Israel's north, often referred to in English as the Sea of Galilee

Knesset (ki-neh-SET)—Israel's legislature

Likud (lee-KOOD)—right-wing political party that favors territorial strength and free markets

Mandatory Palestine (man-dah-TOR-ee pal-ih-STYN)—refers to an area of land in the Middle East under British control from 1922 through 1948

NASDAQ (nehs-DACK)—stands for "National Association of Securities Dealers Automated Quotations;" it is the second largest stock exchange in the world and focuses primarily on technology companies

OECD (oh-ee-cee-dee)—stands for Organization for Economic Cooperation and Development; it's an organization of 34 economically developed countries

Palestinian Authority (PA) (pal-ih-STIH-nee-en aw-THOR-ih-tee)—established in 1994 to govern areas under Palestinian control

Silicon Valley (sih-lih-KAHN val-ee)—nickname for area in and around San Francisco, California where many technology start-ups and companies are located; "silicon" refers to a material used in some computer hardware

Sinai Peninsula (sy-NY peh-NIN-soo-lah)—large desert in Egypt that borders Israel and Gaza in the south

socialism (soh-sha-LIZ-mm)—an economic theory based on common ownership, usually controlled through government, of property and labor

Tel Aviv (tell ah-VEEV)—Israel's largest city, founded in 1909

venture capital (vehn-CHOOR keh-pih-TUL)—money invested in a new business

GLOSSARY

Yiddish (YIH-dish)—a language dating back to the Middle Ages, that had been a primary language spoken by Eastern European Jews until World War II; it is a combination of Hebrew, Aramaic, German, and several Slavic languages

Zionist (ZA-ah-NIZM)—an advocate of Zionism, the philosophy holding that the Jewish people should have a Jewish nation in their ancient homeland; based on the biblical word "Zion," which refers to Jerusalem and Israel

INDEX

PHOTO CREDITS: Design elements from Thinkstock and Dreamstime/Sharon Beck. Cover, p. 1—Brian Cassella/TNS/Newscom; p. 2 (map)—United Nations; pp. 2–3 (background), 4–5, 21, 22, 26 (top), 26–27 (background), 27 (male), 35, 36–37 (background), 39, 40, 44–45 (background), 45 (front, bottom), 48, 50, 52–53 (background)—Thinkstock; p. 8—Zoltan Kluger/Israel's National Photo Collection; p. 11—US Air Force; p. 12—Kibbutz Einat Archive via PikiWiki; pp. 12–13—PikiWiki-Israel/cc-by-2.5; p. 16—Israel Hadari/ZUMAPRESS/Newscom; p. 19—Pallava Bagla/Corbis/APImages; pp. 21 (top, right), 25, 26 (bottom), 36 (top), 36 (bottom), 44 (bottom, front), 45 (top, front)—Lucidwaters/Dreamstime; p. 27 (top)—Zhukovsky/Dreamstime; p. 26 (female)—Barbara Mitchell; pp. 29, 52 (bottom)—Ziv Koren/Polaris/Newscom; p. 31—Rrodrickbeiler/Dreamstime; p. 32—Dnaveh/Dreamstime; p. 37 (top)—Alexandr Makarenko/Dreamstime; p. 37 (bottom)—Alexey Stiop/Dreamstime; p. 42—Konstantin Lanzet/CPU Collection/cc-by-sa-3.0; p. 43—Evan-Amos/Public Domain; p. 44 (top, front)—Eldadcarin/Dreamstime; p. 46—Olga Besnard/Dreamstime; p. 47—Public Domain; p. 52 (top)—Alexirina27000/Dreamstime; p. 53 (bottom)—Leonid Spektor/Dreamstime; p. 55—Oxford Analytical.

About the Author

Elisa Silverman has written a number of books on Israel for Mitchell Lane Publishers. Originally from Chicago, she has lived and worked in Jerusalem, Israel for over a decade. Before becoming a freelance writer, she worked as a client services and project manager for a major contact center in Jerusalem.

Today, Elisa writes business marketing content, and also writes about legal and educational topics. She's graduated from Brandeis University with a bachelor's degree in philosophy and earned a law degree from Emory University School of Law. You can follow Elisa on Twitter @ElisaKapha.